Essential Guide to Writing

Writing Avenue

Michael A. Putlack

Essay Writing

6

 DARAKWON

About the Author

Michael A. Putlack

MA in History, Tufts University, Medford, MA, USA

More than two decades of experience as a writer, editor, and proofreader

Expert test developer of TOEFL, TOEIC, and TEPS

The author of the *Fundamental Reading* Plus series and *Reading Voyage* Starter 2, 3

Essential Guide to Writing

Writing Avenue 6

Essay Writing

Publisher Chung Kyudo
Author Michael A. Putlack
Editors Seo Jeong-ah, Jeong Yeonsoon, Kim Mina, Kim Mikyeong
Designers Park Narae, Forest

First published in March 2021
By Darakwon, Inc.
Darakwon Bldg., 211, Munbal-ro, Paju-si, Gyeonggi-do 10881
Republic of Korea
Tel: 82-2-736-2031 (Ext. 250)
Fax: 82-2-732-2037

ISBN 978-89-277-0452-2 54740
  978-89-277-0446-1 54740 (set)

www.darakwon.co.kr

Photo Credits
mPriceM (p.15), Vorayooth Panakul (p.31), iPIX Stock (p.31), MeAroundtheworld (p.31), Madison Muskopf (p.31), artapartment (p.32), Maridav (p.34), NareshSharma (p.34), SUDONG KIM (p.34), Iakov Filimonov (p.34), jan kranendonk (p.34), NattapolStudiO (p.36), Noushad Thekkayil (p.36), jan kranendonk (p.36), monticello (p.45), DenPhotos (p.54), AngieYeoh (p.55), REDPIXEL.PL (p.57), Art Konovalov (p.64), Paolo Bona (p.71), Iurii Osadchi (p.71), salajean (p.71), CHEN WS (p.71), Neale Cousland (p.71), PhotoStock10 (p.71), Natursports (p.74), muzsy (p.74), Rena Schild (p.74), Hafiz Johari (p.74), Stefan Holm (p.74), Thor Jorgen Udvang (p.74), Melinda Nagy (p.75), katatonia82 (p.75), A_Lesik (p.75), Shahjehan (p.75), Stefan Holm (p.75), New Africa (p.84), OlegDoroshin (p.84), New Africa (p.87) / www.shutterstock.com

Components Main Book / Workbook
10 9 8 7 6 5 4   24 25 26 27 28

Essential Guide to Writing

Writing Avenue

Essay Writing

6

Table of Contents

How to Use This Book

• *Student Book*

1. Before You Write

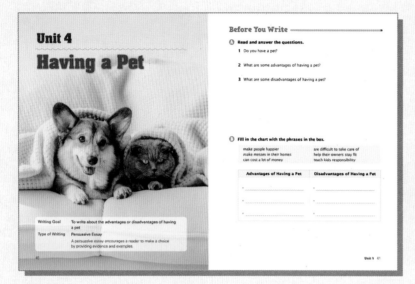

Thinking about the Topic

Three warm-up questions help readers think about the writing topic.

Previewing the Key Expressions

Readers can learn the key expressions by matching the phrases with the pictures or by filling in the table.

2. Analyzing the Model Essay

Reading the Model Essay

Readers can read an example of the essay topic and use it as a template when they write their essay.

Answering Questions

Several questions about the model essay are provided. By answering them, readers can learn the topic of the essay and what important details are included.

QR code for listening to the model essay

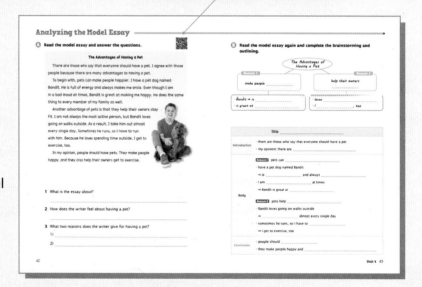

Completing the Brainstorming and Outlining

By completing the brainstorming and outlining, readers can review the model essay and learn how the essay is structured.

3. Collecting Ideas

Getting Ideas from Collecting Ideas

Ideas related to the writing topic are provided. Readers can brainstorm and learn new ideas before writing their drafts.

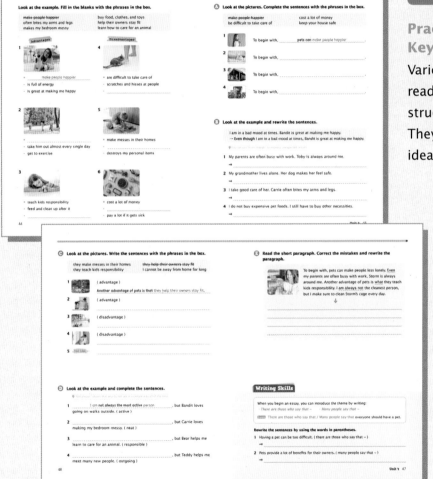

4. Sentence Practice

Practicing Sentences with Key Structures

Various types of questions allow readers to practice the key structures of the model essay. They also help readers gather ideas before writing.

Correcting a Short Paragraph

Readers can check if they understand the key structures they learned by correcting the mistakes in the short paragraph.

5. Writing Skills

Readers learn various phrases and expressions that can help them improve their writing skills.

6. Brainstorming & Outlining

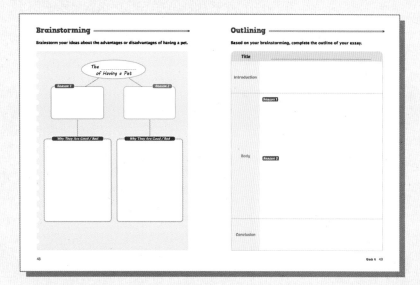

Brainstorming
Readers can come up with ideas about the essay topic.

Outlining
By making an outline, readers can organize their ideas and structure their essays to have an introduction, a body, and a conclusion. Then, they can write, revise, edit the first draft, and write the final draft in the workbook.

Vocabulary and Structure Review
Readers can review the key vocabulary they learned in each unit by writing the meaning of each word and phrase. They can also review the key structures in the unit.

• Workbook

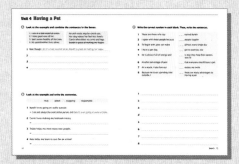

7. More Questions
Readers can practice and review the key structures. They can also write sentences from the model essay by matching the phrases.

8. First Draft → Final Draft
By using the outline, readers can write their first drafts. After revising and editing their drafts, readers can write their final drafts.

About Essay Writing

1. What Is an Essay?

An essay is a short work of writing that is often personal and nonfiction in nature. An essay often describes, argues, explains, or analyzes a particular subject. In an essay, the writer may use facts or personal arguments to make a point.

2. What Does an Essay Consist Of?

An essay consists of three main parts: an introduction, a body, and a conclusion.

- The introduction is the first paragraph of the essay. It introduces the topic of the essay. It also has a thesis statement, which is the main idea of the essay.
- The body is the main part of the essay. It is made up of one or more paragraphs. Each body paragraph has a topic sentence and supporting details.
- The conclusion is the final paragraph of the essay. It summarizes the main points of the essay and restates the thesis.

The Advantages of Having a Pet

Introduction · Thesis Statement

There are those who say that everyone should have a pet. I agree with those people because there are many advantages to having a pet.

To begin with, pets can make people happier. I have a pet dog named Bandit. He is full of energy and always makes me smile. Even though I am in a bad mood at times, Bandit is great at making me happy. He does the same thing to every member of my family as well.

Another advantage of pets is that they help their owners stay fit. I am not always the most active person, but Bandit loves going on walks outside. As a result, I take him out almost every single day. Sometimes he runs, so I have to run with him. Because he loves spending time outside, I get to exercise, too.

In my opinion, people should have pets. They make people happy, and they also help their owners get to exercise.

Body · Conclusion

3. What Are the Types of Essays?

1) Expository Essay

It gives information about a topic or explains how to do something.

2) Narrative Essay

It describes a story that happened to you. It can also describe imaginary events.

3) Persuasive Essay

It encourages readers to make a choice by providing evidence and examples.

4) Descriptive Essay

It describes a person, place, or thing. It shows what the person, location, or object is like.

Unit 1

The House of My Dreams

Writing Goal	To write about my dream house
Type of Writing	Descriptive Essay

A descriptive essay describes a person, place, or thing. It shows the reader what the person, location, or object is like.

Before You Write

A **Read and answer the questions.**

1 Do you have a dream house?

2 Where would your dream house be?

3 What features would your dream house have?

B **Match the pictures with the words or phrases in the box.**

countryside	attic	skylight
patio	theater	cottage

1

2

3

4

5

6

Analyzing the Model Essay

 Read the model essay and answer the questions.

My Dream House

People frequently ask me where I want to live in the future. So I have thought about my dream house very much.

I like nature and want to live a peaceful life. So I wish I had a house in the countryside. My dream house would be located on a large area of land away from any cities. On my land, I want to have plenty of trees, especially fruit trees. I would like to have a pond and a large yard, too.

As for the house itself, my dream house would be a beautiful place with three floors. The house would have many rooms, such as several bedrooms, bathrooms, and living rooms. It would also have a library whose walls are covered with books. Finally, there would be a swimming pool so that I could relax in it.

I wish I could become successful in the future. Then, I would be able to buy my dream house one day.

1 What is the essay about?

_____

2 Why does the writer want to have a house in the countryside?

_____

3 What features would the writer's dream house have?

_____

_____

B **Read the model essay again and complete the brainstorming and outlining.**

```
                        My
                    Dream House

  Feature 1                              Feature 2

    a house in the                        a house with

  _____                       _____

  • on land away from any cities         • have many rooms
  • would have plenty of _____       • would have _____
  • would have _____ and a large     • would be _____
    yard
```

Title _____	
Introduction	• people frequently ask me where I want to live in the future • have thought about my dream house very much
Body	**Feature 1** wish I had a house _____ • would be located _____ • want to have _____ • would like to have _____ **Feature 2** would be _____ • would have _____ • would have _____ • would be _____
Conclusion	• wish I could become successful in the future • would be able to buy my dream house one day

Collecting Ideas

Look at the example. Fill in the blanks with the phrases in the box.

a small cottage
~~a house with three floors~~
a log cabin with a fireplace

an apartment on the top floor
a house with palm trees around it
a large modern house

1

- in the countryside
- _a house with three floors_
- a library and a swimming pool

2

- in the mountains
- _____
- huge windows and a barn

3

- at the beach
- _____
- a big patio and skylights

4

- by a lake
- _____
- an attic and a garden

5

- near a park
- _____
- a theater and a garage

6

- in a city
- _____
- a spacious living room and a gym

Sentence Practice

Ⓐ Look at the pictures. Write the sentences with the phrases in the box.

~~in the countryside~~	at the beach	in the mountains	near a park

💡 Use "I wish + past simple" to express a wish in the present or future.

1   **I wish I had a house** in the countryside. _____

2   _____

3   _____

4   _____

5   Your Idea   _____

Ⓑ Look at the example and write the sentences.

1   a beautiful place / with three floors

→ **As for the house itself, my dream house would be** a beautiful place with three floors.

2   a log cabin / with a fireplace

→ _____

3   an apartment / on the top floor

→ _____

4   a house / with palm trees around it

→ _____

C **Look at the pictures and write the sentences.**

Use "whose" to introduce relative clauses that show possession.

1 (a library / its walls are covered with books)

It would have a library **whose** walls are covered with books.

2 (a living room / its ceiling is very high)

_____

3 (a kitchen / its appliances are modern)

_____

4 (a bedroom / its window overlooks the ocean)

_____

D **Look at the pictures. Complete the sentences with the words in the box.**

| a garden | a swimming pool | a barn | a garage |

Use "so that ~" to provide an explanation for a reason or purpose.

1 (relax)

Finally, _there would be_ a swimming pool **so that I could** relax **in it** .

2 (keep my animals)

Finally, _____ .

3 (grow my own vegetables)

Finally, _____ .

4 (park my cars)

Finally, _____ .

16

E **Read the short paragraph. Correct the mistakes and rewrite the paragraph.**

I wish I <u>have</u> a house at the beach. As for the house itself, my dream house would be a house with palm trees around it. It would also have a big patio <u>which</u> area has a picnic table and a grill. Finally, there would be skylights <u>so as</u> I could see the stars at night.

_____

_____

_____

_____

Writing Skills

When you provide specific examples of something, you can write:

· such as   · like

Example The house would have many rooms, such as / like several bedrooms, bathrooms, and living rooms.

Combine the sentences by using the words in parentheses.

1   My yard would have many trees. It would have coconut trees, palm trees, and mango trees. (such as)

    ➜ _____

2   The apartment would have many facilities. It would have a gym, a café, and an indoor swimming pool. (like)

    ➜ _____

Brainstorming

Brainstorm your ideas about your dream house.

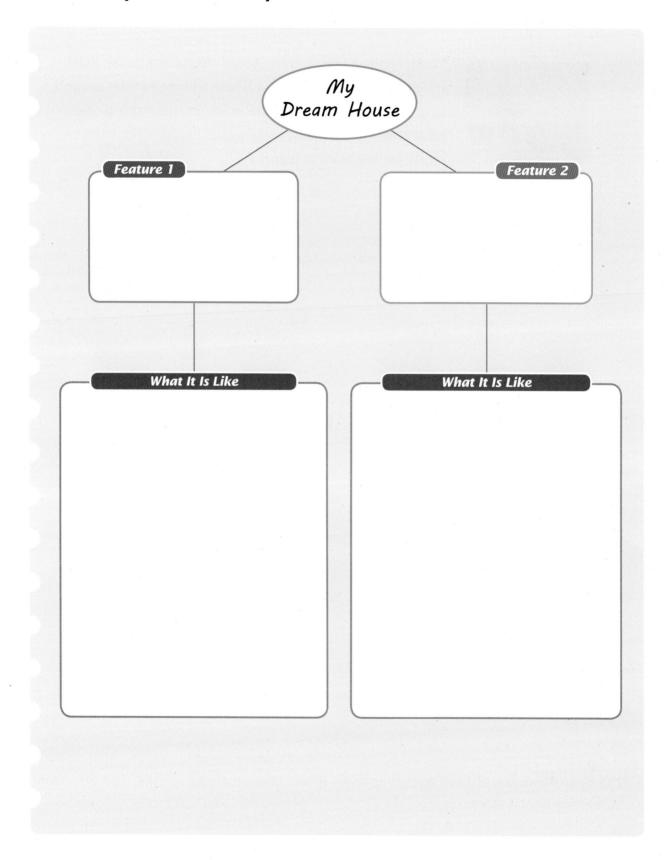

My
Dream House

Feature 1

Feature 2

What It Is Like

What It Is Like

Outlining

Based on your brainstorming, complete the outline of your essay.

Title	
Introduction	
Body	**Feature 1**
	Feature 2
Conclusion	

Unit 2
Health Habits

Writing Goal	To write about my bad health habits
Type of Writing	Narrative Essay
	A narrative essay describes a story that happened to you. It can also describe imaginary events.

Before You Write

A **Read and answer the questions.**

  1 Do you have any bad health habits?

  2 How do these habits affect your health?

  3 How would you like to change these habits?

B **Match the pictures with the correct words and phrases in the box.**

wash my face	stay up late	play video games
exercise	eat junk food	brush my teeth

1

_____

2

_____

3

_____

4

_____

5

_____

6

_____

Analyzing the Model Essay

A **Read the model essay and answer the questions.**

My Bad Health Habits

I have several good habits, but I also have a few bad ones. Unfortunately, many of those bad habits affect my health.

First, I really love to eat junk food. For example, I regularly enjoy food such as chocolate, candy, and potato chips. They taste delicious. However, my bad habit has caused a big problem for me. I am overweight because the junk food has made me gain too much weight.

Another one of my bad habits is that I do not brush my teeth enough. This is a big problem because my diet includes lots of sugar. The last time I went to the dentist, he told me that I had three cavities. I should have brushed my teeth more often.

I used to take good care of my body, but I do not anymore. I have developed some bad health habits. I will try my best to develop better health habits in the future.

1 What is the essay about?

_____

2 What are the writer's two bad health habits?

1) _____

2) _____

3 What problems have those bad health habits caused?

1) _____

2) _____

B Read the model essay again and complete the brainstorming and outlining.

My Bad Health Habits

Habit 1

love to

_____

• enjoy chocolate, candy, and potato chips
• am _____

Habit 2

do not _____
enough

• my diet includes _____
• the dentist told me that I had

_____

Title	_____
Introduction	• have several good habits but also have _____ • many of those bad habits _____
Body	**Habit 1** really love to _____ • regularly enjoy food such as _____ • am overweight because _____ **Habit 2** do not _____ • my diet includes _____ • the dentist told me that _____ → should have _____
Conclusion	• used to _____ but do not anymore • will try my best to _____ in the future

Collecting Ideas

Look at the example. Fill in the blanks with the phrases in the box.

~~gain too much weight~~	do not exercise enough	have three cavities
have lots of pimples	get up late	my eyesight gets worse

1

- eat junk food

  ➜ _____gain too much weight_____

2

- do not brush my teeth enough

  ➜ _____

3

- use my smartphone

  ➜ stay inside a lot

4

- _____

  ➜ my body is in bad shape

5

- stay up late at night

  ➜ _____

6

- do not eat breakfast

  ➜ have little energy before lunch

7

- play video games

  ➜ _____

8

- forget to wash my face before bed

  ➜ _____

Sentence Practice

A **Look at the example and complete the sentences.**

1 (the junk food) → (I / gain too much weight)

→ I am overweight because ___the junk food has made me gain___ too much weight .

2 (staying up late) → (I / get up late)

→ I am late for school because _____ .

3 (my smartphone) → (I / stay inside a lot)

→ I do not play outdoors because _____ .

4 (video games) → (my eyesight / get worse)

→ I have to wear glasses because _____ .

Your Idea

5 _____

B **Look at the pictures. Write the sentences with the phrases in the box.**

| do not eat breakfast | ~~do not brush my teeth enough~~ |
| do not exercise enough | forget to wash my face before bed |

1 **Another one of my bad habits is that I** do not brush my teeth enough.

2 _____

3 _____

4 _____

5 Your Idea _____

C Look at the example and complete the sentences with the words and phrases in the box.

| exercise | wash my face | ~~brush my teeth~~ | eat breakfast |

💡Use "should have + p.p." for something that was a good idea in the past but you did not do.

1 I have three cavities. ___**I should have brushed** my teeth___ more often.

2 I have little energy before lunch. _____ every day.

3 I have lots of pimples. _____ before bed.

4 My body is in bad shape. _____ more often.

5 _____   Your Idea

D Look at the pictures. Complete the sentences with the phrases in the box.

| drink plenty of water | eat healthy foods |
| ~~take good care of my body~~ | spend time outdoors and exercise |

💡"Used to + verb" shows that you did an activity in the past but no longer do it in the present.

1 ___**I used to** take good care of my body___ , but I do not anymore.

2 _____ , but I do not anymore.

3 _____ , but I do not anymore.

4 _____ , but I do not anymore.

E **Read the short paragraph. Correct the mistakes and rewrite the paragraph.**

I have a few bad habits. First, I love to play video games. I have to wear glasses because video games have made my eyesight <u>getting</u> worse. Another one of my bad habits <u>are</u> that I forget to wash my face before bed. I <u>should washed</u> my face more often.

_____

_____

_____

_____

Writing Skills

Before you give an example to support a statement, you can write:

· *For example,*   · *For instance,*

Example I really love to eat junk food. For example, / For instance, I regularly enjoy food such as chocolate, candy, and potato chips.

Rewrite the sentences by using the words in parentheses.

1 I do many activities late at night. I watch TV, chat with friends, and read books. (for example)

→ _____

2 I used to exercise a lot. I jogged, played soccer, and went swimming. (for instance)

→ _____

Brainstorming

Brainstorm your ideas about your bad health habits.

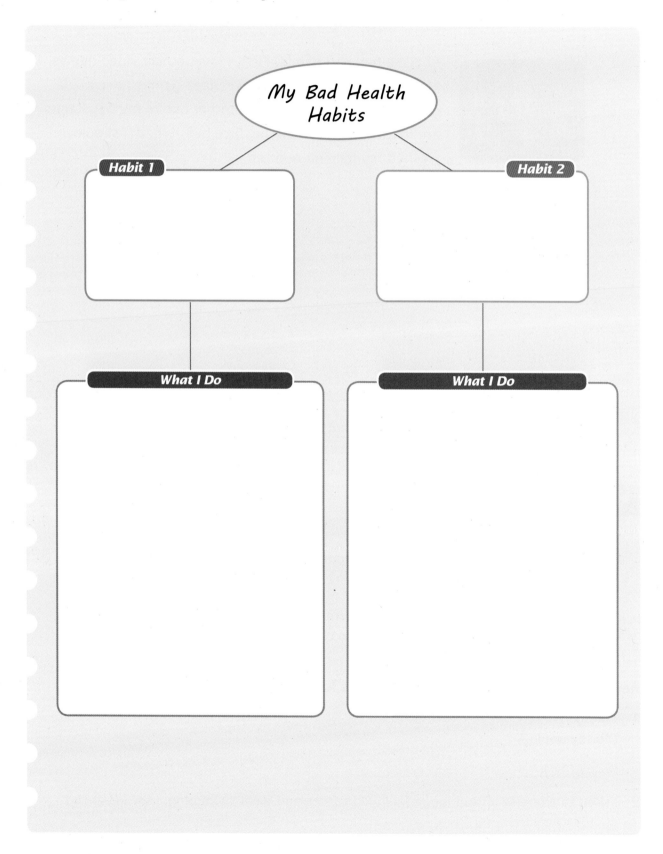

Outlining

Based on your brainstorming, complete the outline of your essay.

Title	
Introduction	
Body	**Habit 1**
	Habit 2
Conclusion	

Unit 3
Popular Festivals

Writing Goal	To write about a popular festival
Type of Writing	Expository Essay

An expository essay gives information about a topic or explains how to do something.

Before You Write

A **Read and answer the questions.**

1 Do you know any popular festivals around the world?

2 When and where do they take place?

3 What activities can people do at them?

B **Match the pictures with the correct festivals in the box.**

Holi   the Quebec Winter Carnival   the Edinburgh Festival Fringe
Songkran   the Boryeong Mud Festival   La Tomatina

1

_____

2

_____

3

_____

4

_____

5

_____

6

_____

Analyzing the Model Essay

 Read the model essay and answer the questions.

Songkran

It is known that Thailand is a beautiful country. One of the best times to visit Thailand is during April. This is when the festival Songkran is held.

Songkran is Thailand's most famous festival. The festival takes place all over the country from April 13 to 15. It is a three-day festival, so many people visit their hometowns. They also visit temples to pray and to give food to monks.

Most people know Songkran as a water festival. During the festival, people throw water on others. Some people even walk around with water guns to shoot others. It is impossible to stay dry during Songkran. What's more, in cities such as Bangkok and Chiang Mai, there are huge water fights. Everyone attending them gets very wet.

Songkran is a fun festival that everyone should try to attend. You will definitely get wet, but you will also have a wonderful time.

1 What is the essay about?

_____

2 When does Songkran take place?

_____

3 Where do many people visit during Songkran?

_____

4 Why do most people know Songkran as a water festival?

_____

B **Read the model essay again and complete the brainstorming and outlining.**

Songkran

Feature 1

_____ most famous festival

• takes place all over the country _____

• a three-day festival → people visit hometowns and _____

Feature 2

a(n) _____ festival

• _____ on others

• walk around with water guns

• there are huge _____ in cities

	Title _____
Introduction	• one of the best times to visit Thailand is _____ • this is when _____
Body	**Feature 1** is _____ • takes place all over the country from April 13 to 15 • is _____ → many people visit their hometowns and also visit temples to _____ **Feature 2** most people know Songkran _____ • people _____ • some people even _____ • in cities such as Bangkok and Chiang Mai, there are _____ → everyone attending them _____
Conclusion	• is a fun festival that everyone should _____ • will definitely _____ but will also have a wonderful time

Collecting Ideas

Look at the example. Fill in the blanks with the phrases in the box.

get into big mud fights
have a big tomato fight
watch canoe races on icy river

~~visit hometowns and temples~~
attend free exhibitions and events
throw colored powder at each other

1
Songkran

- in Thailand / from April 13 to 15
- <u>visit hometowns and temples</u>
- throw water on others

2
the Quebec Winter Carnival

- in Quebec, Canada / from late January to mid-February
- see the ice palace and snow sculptures
- _____

3
Holi

- in India / in March
- celebrate the beginning of spring
- _____

4
the Boryeong Mud Festival

- in Boryeong, Korea / in July
- _____
- enjoy the health benefits of mud

5
La Tomatina

- in Buñol, Spain / on the last Wednesday of August
- _____
- enjoy parades, fireworks, and a paella cooking contest

6
the Edinburgh Festival Fringe

- in Edinburgh, Scotland / in August
- watch various types of performances
- _____

Sentence Practice

A Look at the example and write the sentences.

Use "It is known that ~" to describe something that people know.

1 Thailand / a beautiful country

→ **It is known that** Thailand **is** a beautiful country.

2 Quebec, Canada / an amazing city

→ _____

3 Boryeong, Korea / a fun place

→ _____

4 Edinburgh / the capital of Scotland

→ _____

Your Idea

5 _____

B Look at the example and write the sentences.

1 Thailand / April

→ **One of the best times to visit** Thailand **is during** April.

2 India / spring

→ _____

3 Edinburgh / the summertime

→ _____

4 Quebec / January and February

→ _____

Your Idea

5 _____

C Look at the example and complete the sentences with the phrases in the box.

| a water festival   an ice and snow festival   a festival of colors |

1 Most people know Songkran _____ **as** a water festival _____ .

2 Most people know Holi _____ .

3 Most people know the Quebec Winter Carnival _____ .

D Look at the pictures and write the sentences.

1 (throw water on others)

During the festival, people throw water on others.

2 (throw colored powder at each other)

_____

3 (get into big mud fights)

_____

4 (watch various types of performances)

_____

E Look at the example and rewrite the sentences.

💡 You can use "it" when a "to-infinitive" phrase is the subject of a sentence.

1 To stay dry during Songkran is impossible.

→ **It** is impossible **to stay** dry during Songkran.

2 To throw tomatoes at each other is exciting.

→ _____

3 To watch performances from all over the world is enjoyable.

→ _____

F **Read the short paragraph. Correct the mistakes and rewrite the paragraph.**

It knows that Buñol is a small town in Spain. La Tomatina takes place in Buñol on the last Wednesday of August. Most people know La Tomatina with a food-fight festival. During the festival, people have a big tomato fight. This is exciting to throw tomatoes at each other.

↓

_____

_____

_____

_____

Writing Skills

When you want to provide more information about a topic, you can write:
- *What's more,*   - *Not only that, but ~*

Example During the festival, people throw water on others. What's more, / Not only that, but in cities such as Bangkok and Chiang Mai, there are huge water fights.

Rewrite the sentences by using the words in parentheses.

1 People watch various types of performances. There are free exhibitions and events. (what's more)

→ _____

2 People can take mud baths. They can do mud sliding. (not only that, but)

→ _____

Brainstorming

Brainstorm your ideas about a popular festival.

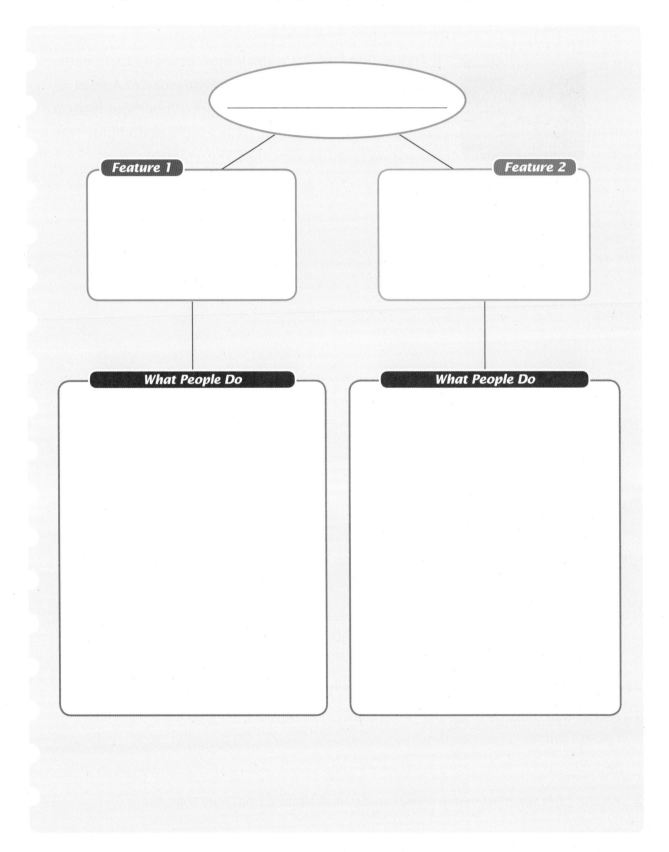

Feature 1

Feature 2

What People Do

What People Do

Outlining

Based on your brainstorming, complete the outline of your essay.

Title	
Introduction	
Body	**Feature 1**
	Feature 2
Conclusion	

Unit 4
Having a Pet

Writing Goal	To write about the advantages or disadvantages of having a pet
Type of Writing	Persuasive Essay
	A persuasive essay encourages a reader to make a choice by providing evidence and examples.

Before You Write

A **Read and answer the questions.**

1 Do you have a pet?

2 What are some advantages of having a pet?

3 What are some disadvantages of having a pet?

B **Fill in the chart with the phrases in the box.**

make people happier	are difficult to take care of
make messes in their homes	help their owners stay fit
can cost a lot of money	teach kids responsibility

Advantages of Having a Pet	Disadvantages of Having a Pet
• _____	• _____
• _____	• _____
• _____	• _____

Analyzing the Model Essay

A   **Read the model essay and answer the questions.**

The Advantages of Having a Pet

There are those who say that everyone should have a pet. I agree with those people because there are many advantages to having a pet.

To begin with, pets can make people happier. I have a pet dog named Bandit. He is full of energy and always makes me smile. Even though I am in a bad mood at times, Bandit is great at making me happy. He does the same thing to every member of my family as well.

Another advantage of pets is that they help their owners stay fit. I am not always the most active person, but Bandit loves going on walks outside. As a result, I take him out almost every single day. Sometimes he runs, so I have to run with him. Because he loves spending time outside, I get to exercise, too.

In my opinion, people should have pets. They make people happy, and they also help their owners get to exercise.

1   What is the essay about?

_____

2   How does the writer feel about having a pet?

_____

3   What two reasons does the writer give for having a pet?

    1) _____

    2) _____

B Read the model essay again and complete the brainstorming and outlining.

The Advantages of Having a Pet

Reason 1

make people _____

• Bandit → is _____
• is great at _____

Reason 2

help their owners
_____

• loves _____
• I _____ , too

Title	_____
Introduction	• there are those who say that everyone should have a pet • my opinion: there are _____
Body	Reason 1 pets can _____ • have a pet dog named Bandit → is _____ and always _____ • I am _____ at times → Bandit is great at _____ Reason 2 pets help _____ • Bandit loves going on walks outside → _____ almost every single day • sometimes he runs, so I have to _____ → I get to exercise, too
Conclusion	• people should _____ • they make people happy and _____

Collecting Ideas

Look at the example. Fill in the blanks with the phrases in the box.

make people happier

buy food, clothes, and toys

often bites my arms and legs

help their owners stay fit

makes my bedroom messy

learn how to care for animals

Advantages

Disadvantages

1

- _____ make people happier _____
- is full of energy
- is great at making me happy

4

- are difficult to take care of
- scratches and hisses at people
- _____

2

- _____
- take him out almost every single day
- get to exercise

5

- make messes in their homes
- _____
- destroys my personal items

3

- teach kids responsibility
- feed and clean up after it
- _____

6

- cost a lot of money
- _____
- pay a lot if it gets sick

Sentence Practice

A **Look at the pictures. Complete the sentences with the phrases in the box.**

~~make people happier~~	cost a lot of money
be difficult to take care of	keep your house safe

1 To begin with, _____ **pets can** make people happier _____.

2 To begin with, _____.

3 To begin with, _____.

4 To begin with, _____.

B **Look at the example and rewrite the sentences.**

I am in a bad mood at times. Bandit is great at making me happy.
→ **Even though** I am in a bad mood at times, Bandit is great at making me happy.

💡 You can use "even though" to express unexpected results.

1 My parents are often busy with work. Toby is always around me.

→ _____

2 My grandmother lives alone. Her dog makes her feel safe.

→ _____

3 I take good care of her. Carrie often bites my arms and legs.

→ _____

4 I do not buy expensive pet food. I still have to buy other necessities.

→ _____

C **Look at the pictures. Write the sentences with the phrases in the box.**

they make messes in their homes	~~they help their owners stay fit~~
they teach kids responsibility	I cannot be away from home for long

1 (advantage)

Another advantage of pets is that they help their owners stay fit.

2 (advantage)

_____

3 (disadvantage)

_____

4 (disadvantage)

_____

5 Your Idea _____

D **Look at the example and complete the sentences.**

💡 "Not always" shows that you do not act in a certain way all of the time.

1 _____ I am **not always the most active** person _____, but Bandit loves going on walks outside. (active)

2 _____, but Carrie loves making my bedroom messy. (neat)

3 _____, but Bear helps me learn to care for animals. (responsible)

4 _____, but Teddy helps me meet many new people. (outgoing)

E **Read the short paragraph. Correct the mistakes and rewrite the paragraph.**

To begin with, pets can make people less lonely. <u>Even</u> my parents are often busy with work, Storm is always around me. Another advantage of pets is <u>what</u> they teach kids responsibility. I <u>am always not</u> the cleanest person, but I make sure to clean Storm's cage every day.

↓

_____

_____

_____

_____

Writing Skills

When you begin an essay, you can introduce the topic by writing:

· *There are those who say that ~*   · *Many people say that ~*

Example There are those who say that / Many people say that everyone should have a pet.

Rewrite the sentences by using the words in parentheses.

1 Having a pet can be too difficult. (there are those who say that ~)

➜ _____

2 Pets provide a lot of benefits for their owners. (many people say that ~)

➜ _____

Brainstorming

Brainstorm your ideas about the advantages or disadvantages of having a pet.

The _____ of Having a Pet

Reason 1

Reason 2

Why They Are Good / Bad

Why They Are Good / Bad

Outlining

Based on your brainstorming, complete the outline of your essay.

Title	
Introduction	
Body	**Reason 1** **Reason 2**
Conclusion	

Unit 5

Social Networking Services

Writing Goal	To write about the good and bad points of social networking services
Type of Writing	Expository Essay
	An expository essay gives information about a topic or explains how to do something.

Before You Write

A **Read and answer the questions.**

1 Do you use any social networking services (SNS)?

2 What are some of the good points of SNS?

3 What are some of the bad points of SNS?

B **Fill in the chart with the words and phrases in the box.**

have fun addictive keep in touch with personal information news updates similar interests cause problems bully

Good Points of SNS	Bad Points of SNS
• _____ friends and family	• is very _____
• meet people with _____	• _____ others on SNS
• get instant _____	• _____ at their jobs or school
• _____ talking to people	• spread _____

Analyzing the Model Essay

A **Read the model essay and answer the questions.**

The Good and Bad Points of SNS

These days, people around the world are using social networking services (SNS) more than ever. In my opinion, these websites have both good and bad points.

As for the benefits, SNS is a great way to keep in touch with friends and family. Many people use SNS like Facebook and Twitter. These websites allow users to post updates on their lives and photos. As a result, people can learn about their friends' lives on their computers or phones.

On the other hand, SNS has quite a few disadvantages. SNS is very addictive. Thus, many people would rather be online than talk to people in real life. Many young people want "likes" on SNS posts, so they care too much about others' opinions. This makes them spend their time trying to please others.

All things considered, SNS has both good and bad points. If people use it properly, however, they can get more benefits from it.

1 What is the essay about?

_____

2 What does the writer say a good point of SNS is?

_____

3 What does the writer say a bad point of SNS is?

_____

B **Read the model essay again and complete the brainstorming and outlining.**

The Good and Bad
Points of SNS

Good Point

_____
friends and family

- post _____ on their lives and
  _____
- can learn about their friends' lives

Bad Point

addictive → people would rather
_____

- want "likes"
  → care about _____
- spend their time trying to
  _____

Title	_____
Introduction	• people around the world are using SNS more than ever • my opinion: these websites have _____
Body	Good Point is a great way to _____ • allow users to _____ • people can learn about their friends' lives _____ Bad Point is very _____ → people would rather be online than _____ • many young people want _____ on SNS posts → they _____ others' opinions • spend their time _____
Conclusion	• SNS has both good and bad points • if people _____, they can get more benefits from it

Collecting Ideas

Look at the example. Fill in the blanks with the phrases in the box.

trying to please others	~~post updates on their lives~~
focus less at work or school	share information about hobbies
learn about events happening	spread personal information

Good Points

Bad Points

1

- keep in touch with friends and family
  - → _post updates on their lives_
  and photos

5

- be online too much
  - → spend their time
  _____

2

- meet people with similar interests
  - → _____

6

- bully others
  - → feel scared to go online

3

- get instant news updates
  - → _____

7

- cause problems at their jobs or school
  - → _____

4

- have fun talking to people
  - → relieve stress by communicating
  with others

8

- _____
  - → their personal information
  becomes public

Sentence Practice

A **Look at the pictures. Complete the sentences with the phrases in the box.**

have fun talking to people	meet people with similar interests
get instant news updates	~~keep in touch with friends and family~~

💡 Use "~ is a great way + to-infinitive" to explain an advantage of something.

1 SNS is a great way _____**to keep** in touch with friends and family_____ .

2 SNS is a great way _____ .

3 SNS is a great way _____ .

4 SNS is a great way _____ .

5 Your Idea _____

B **Look at the example and rewrite the sentences.**

1 These websites let users post updates on their lives and photos.

→ These websites **allow** users **to post** updates on their lives and photos.

2 These websites let users share information about hobbies.

→ _____

3 These websites let users learn about events happening everywhere.

→ _____

4 These websites let users relieve their stress by communicating with others.

→ _____

C **Look at the example and complete the sentences with the phrases in the boxes.**

1. be online	1. talk to people in real life
2. bully others	2. be nice
3. waste their time	3. be productive
4. spread personal information	4. keep it secret

💡 "Would rather *A* than *B*" means you would prefer to do a certain activity instead of another one.

1 SNS is very addictive.

Thus, many people ___**would rather** be online **than** talk to people in real life___ .

2 People are anonymous online.

Thus, many people _____ .

3 People constantly check their SNS.

Thus, they _____ .

4 People care less about others online.

Thus, they _____ .

D **Look at the example and unscramble the words.**

1 trying to / makes / spend their time / please others / this / them

→ **This makes** them **spend** their time trying to please others.

2 them / this / with similar interests / meet / makes / people

→ _____

3 this / at work / makes / focus less / or school / them

→ _____

4 their personal information / this / become public / makes

→ _____

E **Read the short paragraph. Correct the mistakes and rewrite the paragraph.**

Many SNS websites allow users <u>relieve</u> their stress by communicating with others. On the other hand, people care less about others online. So they <u>will rather</u> spread personal information than keep it secret. This makes the personal information <u>to become</u> public.

_____

_____

_____

_____

Writing Skills

When you start a conclusion for your essay, you can write:

· All things considered,   · Taking everything into consideration,

Example All things considereds, / Taking everything into consideration, SNS has both good and bad points.

Rewrite the sentences by using the words in parentheses.

1 The disadvantages of SNS outweigh the advantages. (all things considered)

→ _____

2 People can gain lots of benefits from SNS. (taking everything into consideration)

→ _____

Brainstorming

Brainstorm your ideas about the good and bad points of SNS.

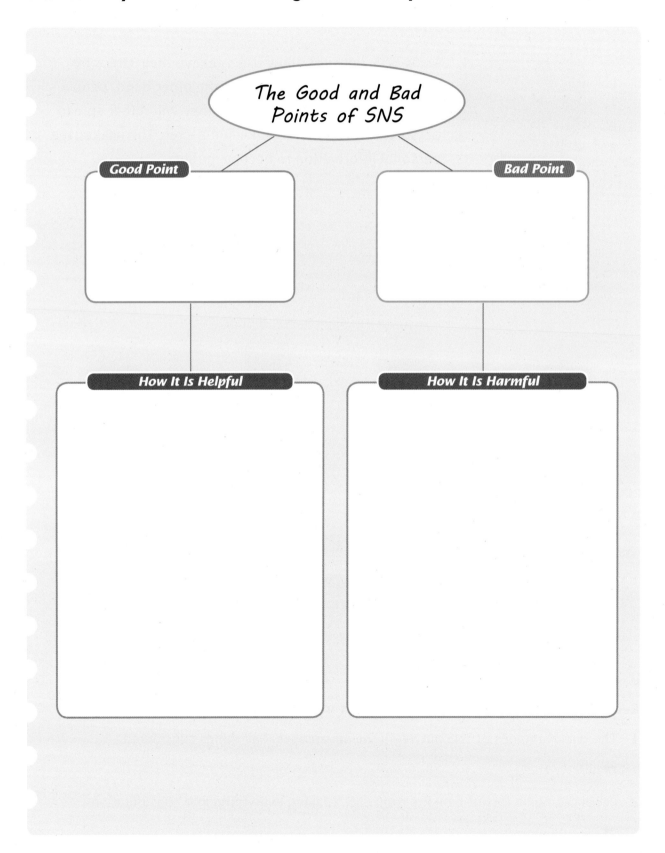

The Good and Bad Points of SNS

Good Point

Bad Point

How It Is Helpful

How It Is Harmful

Outlining

Based on your brainstorming, complete the outline of your essay.

Title	
Introduction	
Body	**Good Point**
	Bad Point
Conclusion	

Unit 6
Traveling

Writing Goal	To write about my preference between two choices
Type of Writing	Persuasive Essay
	A persuasive essay encourages a reader to make a choice by providing evidence and examples.

Before You Write

A **Read and answer the questions.**

1 Do you like to travel?

2 Do you prefer to travel alone or in a group with a tour guide?

3 Why do you like to travel that way?

B **Fill in the chart with the phrases in the box.**

traveling alone	prepare for problems in the future
enjoy clean, fresh air	living in the countryside
saving money	visit every place I want to see

I prefer...	because I can...
• _____	• _____
• _____	• _____
• _____	• _____

Analyzing the Model Essay

A **Read the model essay and answer the questions.**

Traveling Alone

When people take trips, they often travel alone or travel in a group with a tour guide. For me, the choice is simple. I prefer traveling alone to traveling in a group.

First of all, I can visit every place I want to see by traveling alone. For example, I may hear about an interesting place on a trip. Since I am not traveling with a group, I decide to go there. Traveling alone also lets me stay there as long as I want to.

Another reason I travel alone is that I often want to be by myself. I am always surrounded by people when I am not on vacation. So when I take a trip, I want to spend some time alone. Some people think that is boring, but it is refreshing for me.

I like traveling alone better than traveling in a group. I can go anywhere I want to, and I prefer to be by myself.

1 What is the essay about?

_____

2 What is the first reason the writer prefers traveling alone?

_____

3 What is the second reason the writer prefers traveling alone?

_____

B **Read the model essay again and complete the brainstorming and outlining.**

Traveling Alone

Reason 1

can visit

_____

- hear about an interesting place
  → decide to _____
- stay there _____

Reason 2

want to

_____

- am always _____
  → want to spend some time alone
- is _____ for me

Title	_____
Introduction	• people travel alone or travel in a group with a tour guide • I prefer _____ to _____

Body	**Reason 1** can _____ _____
	
	• may hear about _____ on a trip
	
	   → decide to go there
	
	• also _____ as long as I want to
	
	Reason 2 often want to _____
	
	• am always surrounded by people when _____
	
	   → want to _____
	
	• some people think that is boring, but it is _____

Conclusion	• like _____ better than _____ • can go _____ and prefer to be by myself

Collecting Ideas

Look at the example. Fill in the blanks with the phrases in the box.

~~want to be myself~~	buy clothes and electronics
has a lower cost of living	is cheaper than traveling alone
save for future education	use many transportation systems

1

- traveling alone
- visit every place I want to see
- _want to be by myself_

2

- traveling in a group
- visit all kinds of interesting places
- _____

3

- living in a city
- _____
- has many facilities and shops

4

- living in the country
- enjoy clean, fresh air
- _____

5

- spending money
- enjoy my life much better
- like to _____

6

- saving money
- prepare for problems in the future
- need to _____

Sentence Practice

A **Look at the pictures. Complete the sentences with the phrases in the box.**

~~visit every place I want to see~~   enjoy clean, fresh air
prepare for problems in the future   enjoy my life much better

1 (travel alone)

First of all, <u>**I can** visit every place I want to see **by traveling alone**</u> .

2 (live in the country)

First of all, _____.

3 (spend money)

First of all, _____.

4 (save money)

First of all, _____.

B **Look at the example and rewrite the sentences.**

I hear about an interesting place on a trip.
→ **For example, I may** hear about an interesting place on a trip.

💡 Use "may + verb" to express the possibility that something could happen in the future.

1 I want to visit a foreign country.

→ _____

2 I get sick and have to pay a big hospital bill.

→ _____

3 I go to school far away from my house.

→ _____

4 My computer breaks down.

→ _____

C Look at the example and rewrite the sentences.

> I am not traveling with a group. I decide to go there.
> → **Since** I am not traveling with a group, I decide to go there.

💡Use "since" to express a known cause. It means "because."

1 I am traveling with a guide. It is okay not to speak the language there.

→ _____

2 I have money saved. I will not need to worry about the cost.

→ _____

3 There are many types of public transportation. I can go there quickly and easily.

→ _____

4 There are fewer cars on the roads. The air is much cleaner.

→ _____

D Look at the example and write the sentences.

1 (I travel alone.) (I often want to be by myself.)

→ **Another reason** I travel alone **is that** I often want to be by myself.

2 (I like the country.) (It has a lower cost of living.)

→ _____

3 (I save money.) (I need to save for my future education.)

→ _____

4 (I travel in a group) (It is cheaper than traveling alone.)

→ _____

Your Idea

5 _____

E **Read the short paragraph. Correct the mistakes and rewrite the paragraph.**

I prefer saving money to spending money. First of all, I can prepare for problems in the future by <u>save</u> money. For example, my computer may <u>broke down</u>. Since I have money saved, I will not need to worry about the cost. Another reason I save money is <u>because</u> I need to save for my future education.

_____

_____

_____

_____

Writing Skills

When you express a preference, you can write:

· *prefer ~ to...*   · *like ~ better than...*

Example I *prefer* traveling alone *to* traveling in a group.

I *like* traveling alone *better than* traveling in a group.

Write sentences by using the information and words in parentheses.

1 (save money > spend money) (prefer ~ to...)

➡ _____

2 (live in the city > live in the country) (like ~ better than...)

➡ _____

Brainstorming

Brainstorm your ideas about your preference between two choices.

(e.g. traveling alone vs. traveling in a group with a tour guide, living in a city vs. living in the country, spending money vs. saving money)

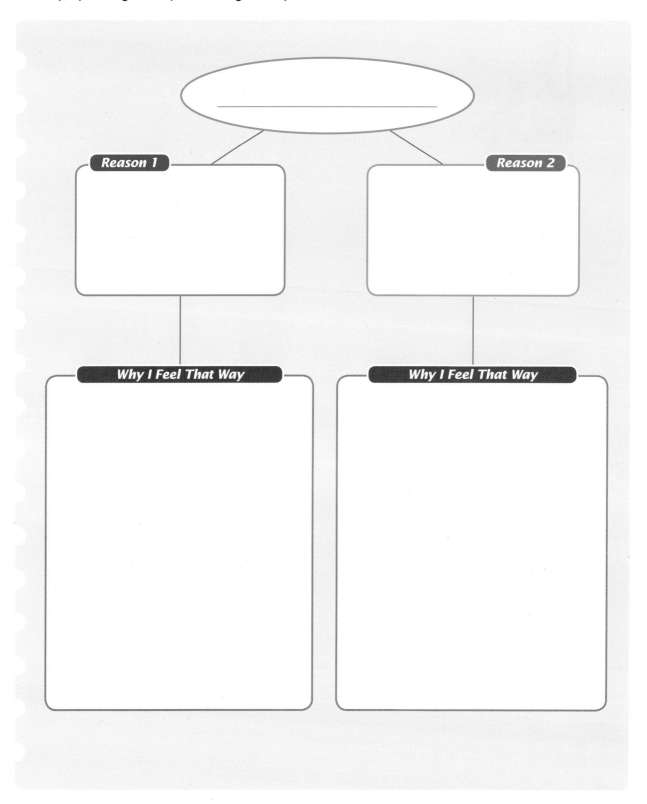

Reason 1

Reason 2

Why I Feel That Way

Why I Feel That Way

Outlining

Based on your brainstorming, complete the outline of your essay.

Title	
Introduction	
Body	**Reason 1**
	Reason 2
Conclusion	

Two Sports

Writing Goal	To write about the similarities and differences between two sports
Type of Writing	Expository Essay
	An expository essay gives information about a topic or explains how to do something.

Before You Write

A **Read and answer the questions.**

1 What are two sports that you know about?

2 How are those two sports similar?

3 How are those two sports different?

B **Match the pictures with the correct phrases in the box.**

play on a court	use a stick	individual sport
hit the ball	team sport	use a racket

1

_____

2

_____

3

_____

4

_____

5

_____

6

_____

Analyzing the Model Essay

A Read the model essay and answer the questions.

Football and Soccer

Two sports many people love are football and soccer. While they are similar in some ways, they are also different.

To start with, both of them are team sports. Like football, a soccer team consists of eleven players on the field at the same time. So the players in each sport must work together as a team to win. In addition, the goal of each sport is to score more than the other team.

Despite their similarities, they also have some differences. In football, players can touch the ball with their hands. However, in soccer, only the goalkeeper can use his hands to touch the ball. Football is also a very physical game. Football players try to tackle the man carrying the ball. On the other hand, soccer is not as physical as football. Soccer players receive a penalty if they hit any players on the other team.

Football and soccer have a few similarities. But they also have some differences.

1 Write two similarities between football and soccer.

1) _____

2) _____

2 Write two differences between football and soccer.

Football	Soccer
Players can touch the ball with their hands.	
	Players receive a penalty if they hit any players on the other team.

B **Read the model essay again and complete the brainstorming and outlining.**

Football and Soccer

Similarities

1) are _____

2) the goal: _____ than the other team

Differences

1) • football: can touch the ball with hands
   • soccer: only _____ can touch the ball

2) • football: try to _____ the man carrying the ball
   • soccer: cannot _____ any players on the other team

Title	_____
Introduction	• two sports many people love • are _____ in some ways but also _____

Body	**Similarities**
	
	1) both of them are _____
	
	  - consists of _____ at the same time
	
	  - must _____ to win
	
	2) the goal of each sport is _____
	
	Differences
	
	1) • football: players can _____
	
	  • soccer: _____ to touch the ball
	
	2) • football: players try to _____
	
	  • soccer: players _____ if they hit any players on the other team

Conclusion	• football and soccer have a few similarities but have some differences

Collecting Ideas

Look at the example. Fill in the blanks with the phrases in the box.

> players use rackets   are played with sticks
> are played on a court   ~~players can touch the ball~~
> are individual or team sports   ride around the field on horses

1

Football vs. Soccer

- Similarity
- - are team sports
- Difference
- - football: <u>players can touch the ball</u> with their hands
- - soccer: only the goalkeeper can use his hands to touch the ball

2

Volleyball vs. Tennis

- Similarity
- - _____
- Difference
- - volleyball: players use their hands to hit the ball
- - tennis: _____ to hit the ball

3

Badminton vs. Ping-Pong

- Similarity
- - _____
- Difference
- - badminton: the shuttlecock cannot hit the ground
- - ping-pong: the ball must hit the table one time

4

Polo vs. Ice Hockey

- Similarity
- - _____
- Difference
- - polo: players _____
- - ice hockey: players move around the ice on skates

Sentence Practice

A **Look at the pictures. Complete the sentences with the phrases in the box.**

~~are team sports~~	are individual or team sports
are played with sticks	are played on a court

1 To start, _____ **both of them** are team sports _____ .

2 To start, _____ .

3 To start, _____ .

4 To start, _____ .

B **Look at the example and complete the sentences.**

use long sticks	has a net in the middle of it
~~consists of eleven players~~	can be played by one or two players

💡 The preposition "like" shows how one thing is similar to another.

1 Like football, a soccer team _____ consists of eleven players _____
   on the field at the same time.

2 Like volleyball, a tennis court _____ .

3 Like badminton, ping-pong _____
   on each side.

4 Like polo, ice hockey players _____ .

C **Look at the example and write the sentences.**

| cannot hit the ground | ride around the field on horses |
| use rackets to hit the ball | ~~can touch the ball with their hands~~ |

1 (football / players)

→ **In football, players** can touch the ball with their hands.

2 (tennis / players)

→ _____

3 (badminton / the shuttlecock)

→ _____

4 (polo / players)

→ _____

Your Idea

5 _____

D **Look at the example and complete the sentences.**

💡 Use "not as ~ as" to make a negative comparison between two people, places, or things.

1 soccer / physical / football

→ On the other hand, _____ soccer **is not as** physical **as** football _____ .

2 ping-pong paddles / long / badminton rackets

→ On the other hand, _____ .

3 ice hockey / old / polo

→ On the other hand, _____ .

4 tennis players / may hit the ball / often / volleyball players

→ On the other hand, _____ .

E **Read the short paragraph. Correct the mistakes and rewrite the paragraph.**

Two sports many people love are polo and ice hockey. To start with, <u>both of they</u> are played with sticks. <u>As</u> polo, ice hockey players use long sticks. Despite their similarities, they also have some differences. Polo is one of the oldest team sports. On the other hand, ice hockey is <u>not as older as</u> polo.

_____

_____

_____

_____

Writing Skills

When you make a contrast between two people, places, or things, you can write:

• _However,_   • _On the other hand,_

Example In football, players can touch the ball with their hands. However, / On the other hand, in soccer, only the goalkeeper can use his hands to touch the ball.

Write sentences by using the information and words in parentheses.

1 (ping-pong – a small, light ball / badminton – a shuttlecock made of feathers) (however)

➡ Ping-pong players use a small, light ball.

_____

2 (polo – four players / ice hockey – six players) (on the other hand)

➡ In polo, there are four players on each team.

_____

Brainstorming

Brainstorm your ideas about similarities and differences between two sports.

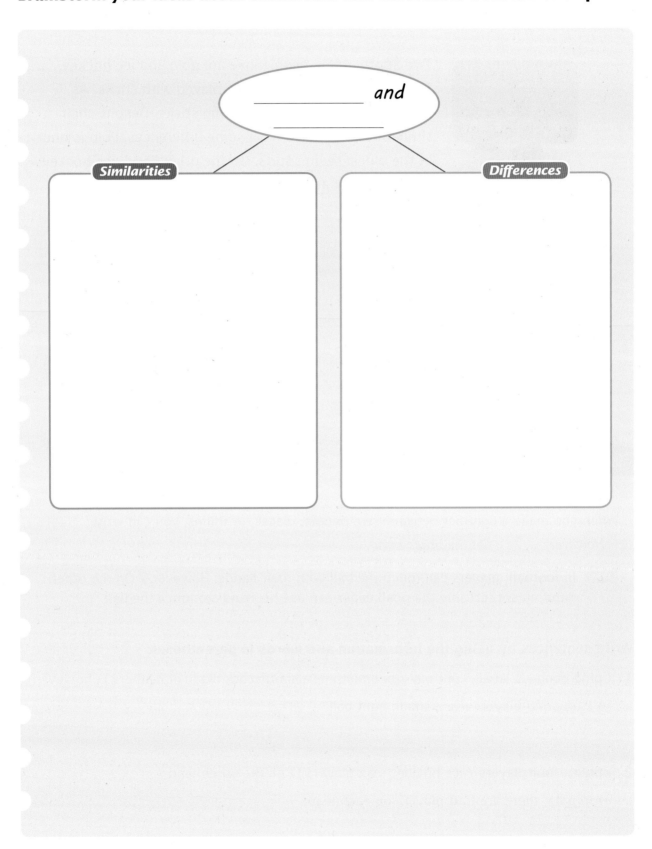

_____ *and*

_____

Similarities

Differences

Outlining

Based on your brainstorming, complete the outline of your essay.

Title	
Introduction	
Body	**Similarities**
	Differences
Conclusion	

Unit 8
Advanced Technology

Writing Goal	To write about the benefits of advanced technology
Type of Writing	Expository Essay
	An expository essay gives information about a topic or explains how to do something.

Before You Write

A **Read and answer the questions.**

1 What are some examples of advanced technology?

2 What do you think the most important type of advanced technology is?

3 How does that type of advanced technology help people?

B **Fill in the chart with the words and phrases in the box.**

| robots | transport goods | computers | communicate with |
| do work | smartphones | airplanes | factories |

Advanced Technology	Benefit
• _____	• work in _____
• _____	• _____ at our jobs
• _____	• _____ other people
• _____	• _____ fast

Analyzing the Model Essay

A **Read the model essay and answer the questions.**

How Robots Make Our Lives Better

We live in a time when technology has a great effect on our lives. This has resulted in robots affecting society very much.

First of all, we use robots to work in factories. Robots can do dangerous, difficult, and dirty work very well. In fact, no people can work harder than robots. Thanks to robots, we can produce all kinds of items quickly and cheaply.

Robots help people another way, too. They can work in places that humans cannot go to. Right now, there are robots deep underwater, inside volcanoes, and even on Mars. Whether the temperature is hot or cold, it does not matter to robots. They can work anywhere. As a result, people do not get hurt while doing some types of work.

Robots are better creations than any other form of technology. They work well in factories and visit places that humans cannot go to, so they make our lives better.

1 What is the essay about?

_____

2 Where do robots work?

1) _____

2) _____

3 How can people benefit from robots in those places?

1) _____

2) _____

B **Read the model essay again and complete the brainstorming and outlining.**

How Robots Make
Our Lives Better

Benefit 1

work in _____

- can do _____
  work very well
- can produce all kinds of items
  _____

Benefit 2

work in places that
_____

- deep underwater, inside volcanoes, and
  even on Mars
- people do not _____
  while doing some types of work

	Title _____
Introduction	• technology has a great effect on our lives • has resulted in _____
Body	**Benefit 1** use robots to _____ • robots can do _____ • we can _____ quickly and cheaply **Benefit 2** robots can work in _____ • there are robots _____ • people do not _____
Conclusion	• are _____ than any other form of technology • _____ and visit places that humans cannot go to → make our lives better

Collecting Ideas

Look at the example. Fill in the blanks with the phrases in the box.

> work in factories
> transport goods fast
> help people be entertained
> do all of the driving
> act like small computers
> make many things cheaply

1

- Robots
- ___work in factories___
- work in places that humans cannot go to

2

- Smartphones
- communicate with other people
- _____

3

- Computers
- do work at our jobs
- _____

4

- 3D printers
- _____
- let people create unique items

5

- Airplanes
- fly around the world
- _____

6

- Self-driving cars
- _____
- reduce the number of car accidents

Sentence Practice

A **Look at the example and complete the sentences.**

1 robots / work in factories

→ First of all, **we use** robots **to work** in factories. .

2 smartphones / communicate with other people

→ First of all, _____ .

3 computers / do work at our jobs

→ First of all, _____ .

4 self-driving cars / do all of the driving

→ First of all, _____ .

Your Idea

5 _____

B **Look at the example and complete the sentences.**

Use "no ~ comparative than..." to make sentences comparing two people, places, or things.

1 (people / work / hard / robots)

→ In fact, **no** people **can** work **harder than** robots. .

2 (devices / let people contact others / well / smartphones)

→ In fact, _____ .

3 (machines / produce things / cheaply / 3D printers)

→ In fact, _____ .

4 (vehicles / fly around the Earth / fast / airplanes)

→ In fact, _____ .

5 (people / drive / smartly / self-driving cars)

→ In fact, _____ .

C **Look at the example and write the sentences.**

robots	do work much more efficiently
computers	~~produce all kinds of items quickly and cheaply~~
airplanes	travel faster and farther
smartphones	talk to friends, family members, and others easily

(In the box, "robots" is struck through.)

1 **Thanks to** robots, **we can** produce all kinds of items quickly and cheaply.

2 _____

3 _____

4 _____

D **Look at the example and write the sentences.**

💡 Use "whether A or B" when there are two choices or possibilities given.

1 The temperature is hot or cold. It does not matter to robots.

→ **Whether** the temperature is hot or cold, it does not matter to robots.

2 People want to send email or surf the Internet. They can do it with their smartphones.

→ _____

3 The design is simple or complex. 3D printers can make it.

→ _____

4 It rains or snows. The weather conditions are not a problem for self-driving cars.

→ _____

E **Read the short paragraph. Correct the mistakes and rewrite the paragraph.**

First of all, we use computers to do work at our jobs. In fact, no people can work <u>fast</u> than computers. <u>Thanks for</u> computers, we can do work much more efficiently. Computers can help people be entertained, too. Whether people want to play games <u>and</u> watch a movie, they can use their computers to do that.

↓

_____

_____

_____

_____

Writing Skills

When you express the effect of an action or event, you can write:

• *result in*   • *lead to*

Example We live in a time when technology has a great effect on our lives. This has resulted in / led to robots affecting society very much.

Rewrite the sentences by using the words in parentheses.

1 Self-driving cars can reduce the number of car accidents. There are fewer injuries.
   (this / will / result in)

   → _____

2 3D printers can make anything there is a design for. People make creative inventions.
   (this / can / lead to)

   → _____

Brainstorming

Brainstorm your ideas about a type of advanced technology and how it helps people.

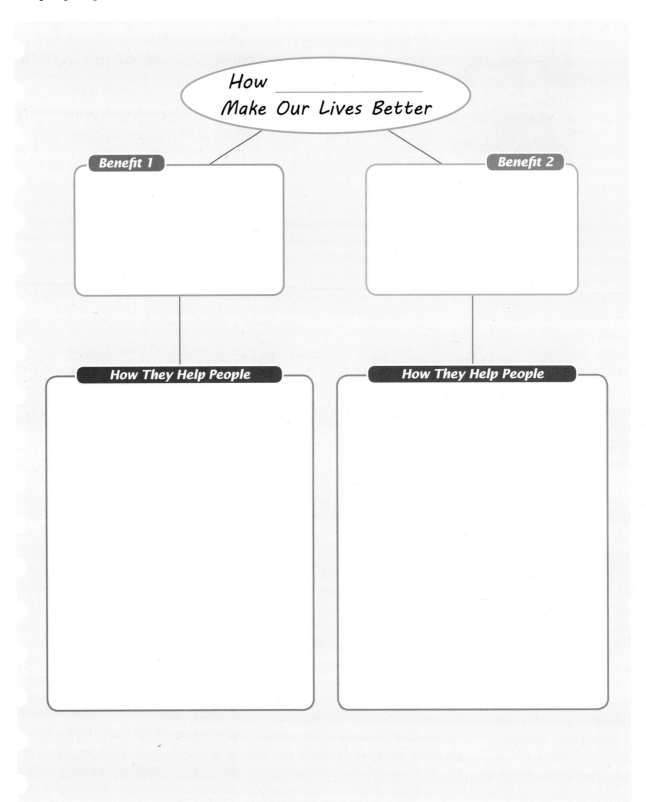

How _____
Make Our Lives Better

Benefit 1

Benefit 2

How They Help People

How They Help People

Outlining

Based on your brainstorming, complete the outline of your essay.

Title	
Introduction	
Body	**Benefit 1**
	Benefit 2
Conclusion	

Vocabulary & Structure Review

Unit 1
The House of My Dreams

Read the words and phrases. Write the meaning next to each word and phrase.

1	countryside		11	skylight	
2	pond		12	cottage	
3	yard		13	attic	
4	floor		14	garage	
5	library		15	apartment	
6	relax (v.)		16	spacious	
7	log cabin		17	gym	
8	fireplace		18	be located	
9	barn		19	as for	
10	patio		20	be covered with	

Structures

1 I wish + past simple

e.g <u>I wish I had</u> a house in the countryside.

<u>I wish I could</u> become successful in the future.

2 the relative pronoun "whose"

e.g It would also have a library <u>whose</u> walls are covered with books.

Unit 2
Health Habits

Read the words and phrases. Write the meaning next to each word and phrase.

1	habit		11	cavity	
2	affect		12	develop	
3	junk food		13	exercise (v.)	
4	regularly		14	eyesight	
5	taste (v.)		15	pimple	
6	cause (v.)		16	gain weight	
7	overweight		17	stay up late	
8	diet		18	brush one's teeth	
9	include		19	take (good) care of	
10	dentist		20	try one's best	

Structures

1 should have + p.p.

   e.g I <u>should have brushed</u> my teeth more often.

2 used to + verb

   e.g I <u>used to take</u> good care of my body, but I do not anymore.

Unit 3
Popular Festivals

Read the words and phrases. Write the meaning next to each word and phrase.

1	during		11	race	
2	hometown		12	icy	
3	temple		13	celebrate	
4	pray		14	mud	
5	monk		15	performance	
6	throw		16	exhibition	
7	shoot		17	definitely	
8	impossible		18	take place (= be held)	
9	attend		19	get wet	
10	sculpture		20	get into a fight (= have a fight)	

Structures

1 It is known that + subject + verb

(e.g) It is known that Thailand is a beautiful country.

2 It ~ to-infinitive

(e.g) It is impossible to stay dry during Songkran.

94

Unit 4
Having a Pet

Read the words and phrases. Write the meaning next to each word and phrase.

1	pet (*n.*)		11	responsibility	
2	advantage (↔ disadvantage)		12	feed	
3	named		13	cost	
4	mood		14	be full of	
5	owner		15	be great at	
6	active		16	stay fit (= keep fit)	
7	hiss		17	go on a walk (= go for a walk)	
8	scratch		18	get to	
9	messy		19	clean up after	
10	destroy		20	make a mess	

Structures

1 even though + subject + verb

e.g Even though I am in a bad mood at times, Bandit is great at making me happy.

2 not always

e.g I am not always the most active person, but Bandit loves going on walks outside.

Unit 5
Social Networking Services

Words & Phrases

Read the words and phrases. Write the meaning next to each word and phrase.

1	allow		11	share (v.)	
2	user		12	hobby	
3	post (v., n.)		13	instant (a.)	
4	update (n.)		14	bully (v.)	
5	addictive		15	scared	
6	care (v.)		16	spread	
7	please (v.)		17	public (↔ personal)	
8	properly		18	keep in touch with	
9	similar		19	go online	
10	interest		20	relieve stress	

Structures

1 ~ is a great way + to-infinitive

e.g SNS <u>is a great way to keep</u> in touch with friends and family.

2 would rather A than B

e.g Thus, many people <u>would rather</u> be online <u>than</u> talk to people in real life.

Unit 6
Traveling

Read the words and phrases. Write the meaning next to each word and phrase.

1	tour guide		11	save	
2	prefer		12	education	
3	interesting		13	take a trip (= travel)	
4	boring		14	decide to	
5	refreshing		15	by oneself (= alone)	
6	cheap		16	be surrounded by	
7	transportation system		17	be on vacation	
8	facility		18	cost of living	
9	clothes		19	prepare for	
10	electronics		20	break down	

1 may + verb

e.g For example, I <u>may hear</u> about an interesting place on a trip.

2 since + subject + verb

e.g <u>Since</u> I am not traveling with a group, I decide to go there.

Unit 7
Two Sports

Read the words and phrases. Write the meaning next to each word and phrase.

1	football		11	difference (*a.* different)	
2	volleyball		12	physical	
3	ping-pong (= table tennis)		13	tackle (*v.*)	
4	while (*conj.*) (= although)		14	penalty	
5	goalkeeper		15	individual (↔ team)	
6	field		16	shuttlecock	
7	court		17	racket	
8	score (*v.*)		18	stick	
9	despite		19	paddle	
10	similarity (*a.* similar)		20	consist of	

1 the preposition "like"

e.g <u>Like</u> football, a soccer team consists of eleven players on the field at the same time.

2 not as ~ as

e.g On the other hand, soccer is <u>not as physical as</u> football.

98

Unit 8
Advanced Technology

Read the words and phrases. Write the meaning next to each word and phrase.

1	advanced technology		11	entertain	
2	factory		12	unique	
3	produce (v.)		13	transport (v.)	
4	underwater (ad.)		14	goods	
5	volcano		15	reduce	
6	Mars		16	self-driving car	
7	temperature		17	have an effect on	
8	matter (v.)		18	result in (= lead to)	
9	creation		19	thanks to	
10	act		20	get hurt	

Structures

1 no ~ comparative than…

e.g In fact, <u>no</u> people can work <u>harder than</u> robots.

2 whether A or B

e.g <u>Whether</u> the temperature is hot <u>or</u> cold, it does not matter to robots.

Memo

Memo

Memo

Memo

Essential Guide to Writing

Writing Avenue

Workbook

Essay Writing

6

DARAKWON

Essential Guide to Writing

Writing Avenue

Workbook

Essay Writing

6

DARAKWON

Unit 1 The House of My Dreams

A Look at the example and write the sentences.

1 (in the countryside)

→ **I wish I had a house** in the countryside.

2 (in the forest)

→ _____

3 (on a tropical island)

→ _____

4 (in a city)

→ _____

B Look at the example and write the sentences.

1 It would also have a library. The library's walls are covered with books.

→ It would also have a library **whose** walls are covered with books.

2 It would also have a living room. The living room's walls have beautiful paintings.

→ _____

3 It would also have a kitchen. The kitchen's appliances are modern.

→ _____

4 It would also have a gym. The gym's equipment is free to use.

→ _____

2

C **Write the correct number in each blank. Then, write the sentences.**

1	People frequently ask me	_____	so that I could relax in it
2	So I have thought about	_____	of trees, especially fruit trees
3	My dream house would be located	_____	my dream house very much
4	On my land, I want to have plenty	_____	buy my dream house one day
5	As for the house itself, my dream house	_____	where I want to live in the future
6	The house would have many rooms, such as	_____	on a large area of land away from any cities
7	Finally, there would be a swimming pool	_____	would be a beautiful place with three floors
8	Then, I would be able to	_____	several bedrooms, bathrooms, and living rooms

1 _____

2 _____

3 _____

4 _____

5 _____

6 _____

7 _____

8 _____

First Draft

Write the first draft by using the outline. Then, revise and edit your essay.

Title	
Introduction	
Body	
Conclusion	

Revising Checklist

1. Did you explain where your dream house would be? ☐
2. Did you write what features your dream house would have? ☐
3. Did you use "I wish + past simple" and the relative pronoun "whose"? ☐

Editing Checklist　　Capitalization ☐　　Punctuation ☐　　Grammar ☐　　Spelling ☐

Final Draft

Write the final draft.

Title _____

Unit 2 **Health Habits**

A **Look at the example and write the sentences.**

1 (brush my teeth / more often)

→ **I should have brushed** my teeth more often. _____

2 (eat fruits and vegetables / more often)

→ _____

3 (go to bed / earlier)

→ _____

4 (wash my face / before bed)

→ _____

B **Look at the example and write the sentences.**

I took good care of my body in the past, but I do not anymore.
→ **I used to take** good care of my body, but I do not anymore.

1 I drank plenty of water in the past, but I do not anymore.

→ _____

2 I brushed my teeth at least twice a day in the past, but I do not anymore.

→ _____

3 I avoided eating sweets in the past, but I do not anymore.

→ _____

4 I went to the gym every other day in the past, but I do not anymore.

→ _____

C **Write the correct number in each blank. Then, write the sentences.**

1	I have several good habits,	_____	bad habits affect my health
2	Unfortunately, many of those	_____	a big problem for me
3	For example, I regularly enjoy food	_____	but I also have a few bad ones
4	However, my bad habit has caused	_____	better health habits in the future
5	I am overweight because the junk food	_____	that I do not brush my teeth enough
6	Another one of my bad habits is	_____	has made me gain too much weight
7	The last time I went to the dentist,	_____	he told me that I had three cavities
8	I will try my best to develop	_____	such as chocolate, candy, and potato chips

1 _____

2 _____

3 _____

4 _____

5 _____

6 _____

7 _____

8 _____

First Draft

Write the first draft by using the outline. Then, revise and edit your essay.

Title	
Introduction	
Body	
Conclusion	

1. Did you write two bad health habits of yours and their details? ☐
2. Did you explain how these habits affect your health? ☐
3. Did you use "should have + p.p." and "used to + verb"? ☐

Capitalization ☐   Punctuation ☐   Grammar ☐   Spelling ☐

Final Draft

Write the final draft.

Title _____

Unit 3 Popular Festivals

A **Look at the example and rewrite the sentences.**

1 People know that Thailand is a beautiful country.

→ **It is known that** Thailand is a beautiful country.

2 People know that India is a very large country.

→ _____

3 People know that Boryeong, Korea, is a fun place.

→ _____

4 People know that Bunõl is a small town in Spain.

→ _____

B **Look at the example and write the sentences.**

1 │ impossible / stay dry / during Songkran │

→ **It is** impossible **to stay** dry during Songkran.

2 │ fun / watch canoe races / on the icy river │

→ _____

3 │ exciting / throw tomatoes / at each other │

→ _____

4 │ easy / do many activities / during the festival │

→ _____

C **Write the correct number in each blank. Then, write the sentences.**

1	One of the best times to visit	_____	water on others
2	The festival takes place	_____	a water festival
3	They also visit temples to pray	_____	Thailand is during April
4	Most people know Songkran as	_____	and to give food to monks
5	During the festival, people throw	_____	water guns to shoot others
6	Some people even walk around with	_____	that everyone should try to attend
7	What's more, in cities such as Bangkok	_____	all over the country from April 13 to 15
8	Songkran is a fun festival	_____	and Chiang Mai, there are huge water fights

1 _____

2 _____

3 _____

4 _____

5 _____

6 _____

7 _____

8 _____

First Draft

Write the first draft by using the outline. Then, revise and edit your essay.

Title	
Introduction	
Body	
Conclusion	

Revising Checklist

1. Did you explain when and where the festival takes place? ☐
2. Did you write two of the main features of the festival and their details? ☐
3. Did you use "It is known that ~" and "It ~ to-infinitive"? ☐

Editing Checklist   Capitalization ☐   Punctuation ☐   Grammar ☐   Spelling ☐

12

Final Draft

Write the final draft.

Title _____

Unit 4 Having a Pet

A Look at the example and combine the sentences in the boxes.

1. ~~I am in a bad mood at times.~~
2. I take good care of her.
3. Spot seems healthy all the time.
4. My grandmother lives alone.

He still needs regular checkups.
Her dog makes her feel less lonely.
Carrie often bites my arms and legs.
~~Bandit is great at making me happy.~~

1 **Even though** I am in a bad mood at times, Bandit is great at making me happy.

2 _____

3 _____

4 _____

B Look at the example and write the sentences.

neat	~~active~~	outgoing	responsible

1 Bandlt loves going on walks outside.

→ **I am not always the most active person, but** Bandit loves going on walks outside.

2 Carrie loves making my bedroom messy.

→ _____

3 Teddy helps me meet many new people.

→ _____

4 Bear helps me learn to care for animals.

→ _____

14

C Write the correct number in each blank. Then, write the sentences.

1	There are those who say	_____	named Bandit
2	I agree with those people because	_____	people happier
3	To begin with, pets can make	_____	almost every single day
4	I have a pet dog	_____	get to exercise, too
5	He is always full of energy and	_____	is that they help their owners stay fit
6	Another advantage of pets	_____	that everyone should have a pet
7	As a result, I take him out	_____	makes me smile
8	Because he loves spending time outside, I	_____	there are many advantages to having a pet

1 _____

2 _____

3 _____

4 _____

5 _____

6 _____

7 _____

8 _____

First Draft

Write the first draft by using the outline. Then, revise and edit your essay.

Title	
Introduction	
Body	
Conclusion	

Revising Checklist

1. Did you explain what you think about people having pets in the introduction? ☐
2. Did you write two reasons to support your opinion and their details? ☐
3. Did you use the conjunction "even though" and "not always"? ☐

Editing Checklist   Capitalization ☐   Punctuation ☐   Grammar ☐   Spelling ☐

16

Final Draft

Write the final draft.

Title _____

Unit 5 Social Networking Services

A **Look at the example and write the sentences.**

1 keep in touch with friends and family

→ **SNS is a great way to** keep in touch with friends and family.

2 make new friends

→ _____

3 share and exchange ideas

→ _____

4 connect with people all around the world

→ _____

B **Look at the example and complete the sentences.**

1 be online / talk to people in real life

→ People _____ **would rather** be online **than** talk to people in real life _____ .

2 bully others / be nice

→ People _____ .

3 waste their time / do something useful

→ People _____ .

4 spread personal information / keep it secret

→ People _____ .

C **Write the correct number in each blank. Then, write the sentences.**

1 These days, people around the world are

_____ both good and bad points

2 Many people use SNS

_____ their time trying to please others

3 These websites allow users to

_____ like Facebook and Twitter

4 As a result, people can learn about their

_____ they can get more benefits from it

5 Many young people want "likes" on SNS posts,

_____ post updates on their lives and photos

6 This makes them spend

_____ so they care too much about others' opinions

7 All things considered, SNS has

_____ using social networking services (SNS) more than ever

8 If people use it properly, however,

_____ friends' lives on their computers or phones

1 _____

2 _____

3 _____

4 _____

5 _____

6 _____

7 _____

8 _____

First Draft

Write the first draft by using the outline. Then, revise and edit your essay.

Title	_____
Introduction	
Body	
Conclusion	

20

Final Draft

Write the final draft.

Title _____

Unit 6 Traveling

A **Look at the example and write the sentences with the phrases in the box.**

have to quit my job	go to a place far away from my house
~~hear about an interesting place~~	want to go to a concert with my friend

1 I can visit every place I want to see by traveling alone.

For example, _____**I may** hear about an interesting place_____ .

2 I can enjoy my life much better by spending money.

For example, _____ .

3 I can prepare for problems in the future by saving money.

For example, _____ .

4 I can use many different transportation systems in the city.

For example, _____ .

B **Look at the example and rewrite the sentences.**

1 I am not traveling with a group. I decide to go there.

→ **Since** I am not traveling with a group, I decide to go there. _____

2 Traveling brings me great joy. I spend money on it.

→ _____

3 The pace of life is slower in the country. It is more peaceful.

→ _____

4 There are more job opportunities in a city. It is easier to find a job.

→ _____

22

ⓒ Write the correct number in each blank. Then, write the sentences.

1	I prefer traveling alone	_____	than traveling in a group
2	Traveling alone also lets me	_____	to traveling in a group
3	Another reason I travel alone	_____	but it is refreshing for me
4	I am always surrounded	_____	stay there as long as I want to
5	So when I take a trip,	_____	and I prefer to be by myself
6	Some people think that is boring,	_____	is that I often want to be by myself
7	I like traveling alone better	_____	by people when I am not on vacation
8	I can go anywhere I want to,	_____	I want to spend some time alone

1 _____

2 _____

3 _____

4 _____

5 _____

6 _____

7 _____

8 _____

First Draft

Write the first draft by using the outline. Then, revise and edit your essay.

Title	
Introduction	
Body	
Conclusion	

Revising Checklist

1. Did you explain what your preference is? ☐
2. Did you write two reasons for your preference and their details? ☐
3. Did you use the conjunction "since" and "may"? ☐

Editing Checklist   Capitalization ☐   Punctuation ☐   Grammar ☐   Spelling ☐

Final Draft

Write the final draft.

Title	_____

Unit 7 Two Sports

A Look at the example and write the sentences.

1   A football team consists of eleven players on the field at the same time. (soccer)

→ **Like football, a soccer team** consists of eleven players on the field at the same time.

2   A volleyball court has a net in the middle of it. (tennis)

→ _____

3   Badminton can be played as singles or doubles. (ping-pong)

→ _____

4   Polo players move around a lot during a game. (ice hockey)

→ _____

B Look at the example and complete the sentences.

| old | big | long | ~~physical~~ |

1   Soccer ___ **is not as** physical **as** ___ football.

2   Ping-pong paddles _____ badminton rackets.

3   Ice hockey _____ polo.

4   A tennis ball _____ a volleyball.

26

C **Write the correct number in each blank. Then, write the sentences.**

1	Two sports many people	_____	carrying the ball
2	To start with, both of	_____	them are team sports
3	So the players in each sport must	_____	the ball with their hands
4	In addition, the goal of each sport	_____	love are football and soccer
5	Despite their similarities,	_____	work together as a team to win
6	In football, players can touch	_____	they also have some differences
7	Football players try to tackle the man	_____	is to score more than the other team
8	Soccer players receive a penalty	_____	if they hit any players on the other team

1 _____

2 _____

3 _____

4 _____

5 _____

6 _____

7 _____

8 _____

First Draft

Write the first draft by using the outline. Then, revise and edit your essay.

Title	
Introduction	
Body	
Conclusion	

1. Did you mention two sports that have similarities and differences? ☐
2. Did you provide similarities and differences for each sport? ☐
3. Did you use the preposition "like" and "not as ~ as"? ☐

Editing Checklist Capitalization ☐ Punctuation ☐ Grammar ☐ Spelling ☐

Final Draft

Write the final draft.

Title _____

Unit 8 Advanced Technology

A Look at the example and unscramble the words.

1 | can / than / no people / robots / work harder |

→ In fact, *no people can work harder than robots*   .

2 | no / produce things / than / 3D printers / machines can / more cheaply |

→ In fact,   .

3 | no vehicles / fly around the Earth / airplanes / can / faster than |

→ In fact,   .

4 | can / people / than self-driving cars / no / more smartly / drive |

→ In fact,   .

B Look at the example and complete the sentences.

1 (the temperature / hot / cold)

→ __**Whether** the temperature is hot **or** cold__ , it does not matter to robots.

2 (people want to / play games / listen to music)

→   , they can use their computers.

3 (the design / simple / complex)

→   , their 3D printers can make it.

4 (it / rains / snows)

→   , the weather conditions are
not a problem to self-driving cars.

C **Write the correct number in each blank. Then, write the sentences.**

1 We live in a time when   _____ work in factories

2 This has resulted in robots   _____ affecting society very much

3 First of all, we use robots to   _____ hurt while doing some types of work

4 Thanks to robots, we can produce   _____ inside volcanoes, and even on Mars

5 Right now, there are robots deep underwater,   _____ than any other form of technology

6 As a result, people do not get   _____ all kinds of items quickly and cheaply

7 Robots are better creations   _____ technology has a great effect on our lives

8 They work well in factories and visit places   _____ that humans cannot go to, so they make our lives better

1 _____

2 _____

3 _____

4 _____

5 _____

6 _____

7 _____

8 _____

First Draft

Write the first draft by using the outline. Then, revise and edit your essay.

Title	
Introduction	
Body	
Conclusion	

Revising Checklist

1. Did you explain what type of advanced technology you think affects our lives very much? ☐
2. Did you write two ways that this type of advanced technology benefits people? ☐
3. Did you use "no ~ comparative than..." and "whether A or B"? ☐

Editing Checklist   Capitalization ☐   Punctuation ☐   Grammar ☐   Spelling ☐

Final Draft

Write the final draft.

Title _____

Memo

Memo